Stratford Library Association
2203 Main Street
Stratford, CT 06615
203-385-4160

 W9-AJK-891

MYSTERIES OF SCIENCE

THE LOCH NESS MONSTER

THE UNSOLVED MYSTERY

BY CONNIE COLWELL MILLER

Reading Consultant:
Barbara J. Fox
Reading Specialist
North Carolina State University

Content Consultant:
Adrian Shine
Loch Ness Project
Inverness-shire, Scotland

Capstone
press

Mankato, Minnesota

Blazers is published by Capstone Press,
151 Good Counsel Drive, P.O. Box 669, Mankato, Minnesota 56002.
www.capstonepress.com

012010
005661R

Library of Congress Cataloging-in-Publication Data
Miller, Connie Colwell, 1976–
    Loch Ness monster: the unsolved mystery/by Connie Colwell Miller.
    p. cm. — (Blazers. Mysteries of science)
    Includes bibliographical references and index.
    Summary: "Presents the legend of the Loch Ness monster, including current theories
and famous sightings" — Provided by publisher.
    ISBN-13: 978-1-4296-2328-5 (hardcover)
    ISBN-10: 1-4296-2328-4 (hardcover)
    1. Loch Ness monster — Juvenile literature. I. Title. II. Series
QL89.2.L6M55 2009
001.944 — dc22   2008028698

Editorial Credits
Lori Shores, editor; Alison Thiele, designer; Marcie Spence, photo researcher

Photo Credits
Alamy/INTERFOTO Pressebildagentur, 16–17
Corbis/Mc Pherson Colin, 4–5; Ralph White, 22; Sam Forencich/Solus-Veer, 28–29; Vo Trung
    Dung, 6–7
Fortean Picture Library, 8–9, 10–11, 24–25
Getty Images Inc./Hulton Archive/Keystone, 20–21; Ian Tyas/Stringer, 12–13; Tom Stoddart,
    26–27
GLOBE PHOTOS, INC., 14–15
Maralyn Shine, 23
Shutterstock/Christian Darkin, cover; Marilyn Volan, grunge background (throughout); Maugli,
    18-19 (background); rgbspace, (paper art element) 3, 19; Shmeliova Natalia, 18 (paper art
    element)

TABLE OF CONTENTS

A NESSIE SIGHTING

One morning in 1934, Margaret Munro began work for the day. The young maid looked out the window at the **loch**.

loch — the Scottish word for lake

Suddenly, a huge animal appeared at the edge of the loch. Its long neck held up a tiny head. It had **flippers** instead of legs.

flipper — one of the broad, flat limbs of a sea creature

Margaret watched as the animal swam back under the water. Margaret had seen the Loch Ness Monster!

NESSIE FACT

People sometimes call the Loch Ness Monster "Nessie."

Some people think this photo, taken in 1933, shows Nessie turning over in the water.

NESSIE
FACT

Stories of the Loch Ness
Monster go back 1,500 years.

THE LOCH NESS MONSTER

Loch Ness is a long, deep lake in Scotland. Many people believe they have seen a **mysterious** beast at Loch Ness.

mysterious — hard to explain or understand

Workers built a road along
Loch Ness in 1933. Nessie **sightings**
became more common as people used
the new road.

sighting — an experience of seeing something

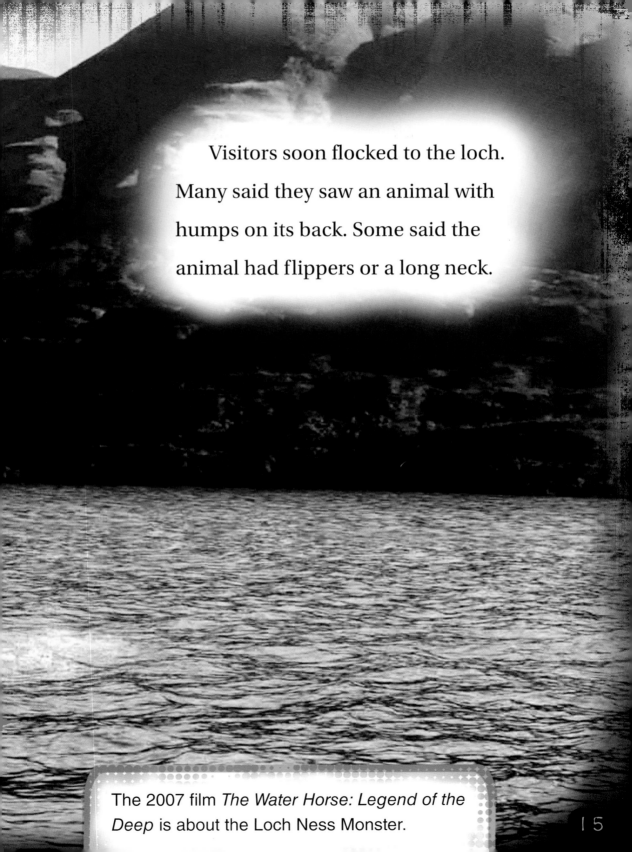

Visitors soon flocked to the loch. Many said they saw an animal with humps on its back. Some said the animal had flippers or a long neck.

The 2007 film *The Water Horse: Legend of the Deep* is about the Loch Ness Monster.

Some people think that Nessie could be a plesiosaur. A plesiosaur was a large dinosaur that lived in and near water.

Many people believe Nessie is a **mammal** such as a whale. Others say that the monster isn't even real.

mammal — a warm-blooded animal that breathes air

FAMOUS SIGHTINGS

In 1933, Mr. and Mrs. John Mackay reported one of the first modern sightings. They watched Nessie roll in the water for more than a minute.

In 1960, Tim Dinsdale recorded the Loch Ness Monster on film. The creature seemed to be about 15 feet (4.6 meters) long. But some people say the moving object was just a boat.

Arthur Grant said he saw Nessie on land in 1934. He almost ran into Nessie with his motorcycle. Grant said the animal was large and had a long neck.

In 1972, scientist Robert Rines used an underwater camera at Loch Ness. One picture showed a flipper-shaped object. Rines thought the object was about 6 to 8 feet (1.8 to 2.4 meters) long.

IS NESSIE REAL?

Some **witnesses** have taken pictures of Nessie. But some of the pictures turned out to be fakes.

witness — a person who has seen or heard something

In 1993, Christian Spurling said he faked this famous picture. The object was only a toy submarine.

NESSIE
FACT

The 1987 sonar test
"Operation Deepscan"
used 19 boats to study
the lake.

Scientists have used **sonar** to look for Nessie. In 1987, a sonar test showed three large objects in the loch. But other sonar tests showed nothing.

sonar — a device that uses sound waves to find underwater objects

Some scientists think that Nessie might just be floating logs. Underwater waves make logs seem to swim on top of the water.

NESSIE FACT

In 1933, someone used a stuffed hippopotamus foot to make fake Nessie footprints.

THE FUTURE OF NESSIE

Skeptics question if Nessie is real.
No one has ever found bones or
remains near the loch.

skeptic — a person who questions things that other people believe in

LOWRANCE

26

NESSIE FACT

Some animals weren't discovered until the 1900s. Even today, new animals are being discovered.

27

People still wonder about the
Loch Ness Monster. Only time will
tell if Nessie is real.

GLOSSARY

flipper (FLIP-ur) — one of the broad, flat limbs of a sea creature

loch (LAHK) — the Scottish word for lake

mammal (MAM-uhl) — a warm-blooded animal that has a backbone and breathes air

mysterious (miss-TIHR-ee-uhss) — hard to explain or understand

sighting (SITE-ing) — an experience of seeing something

skeptic (SKEP-tik) — a person who questions things that other people believe in

sonar (SOH-nar) — a device that uses sound waves to find underwater objects; sonar stands for sound navigation and ranging.

witness (WIT-niss) — a person who has seen or heard something

READ MORE

DeMolay, Jack. *The Loch Ness Monster: Scotland's Mystery Beast.* Jr. Graphic Mysteries. New York: Rosen, 2007.

Shine, Maralyn. *Young Loch Ness Explorers.* Inverness, Scotland: Loch Ness Project, 2008.

Wallace, Holly. *The Mystery of the Loch Ness Monster.* Can Science Solve? Chicago: Heinemann, 2006.

INTERNET SITES

FactHound offers a safe, fun way to find educator-approved Internet sites related to this book.

Here's what you do:

1. Visit *www.facthound.com*
2. Choose your grade level.
3. Begin your search.

This book's ID number is 9781429623285.

FactHound will fetch the best sites for you!

INDEX